FEAR NOT

You Have a Better Standing

SEGUN T. OBADIMU

Copyright © 2017. All rights reserved.

No part of this publication may be reproduced, stored in a retrieval system or transmitted in any way by any means, electronic, mechanical, photocopy, recording or otherwise, without the prior permission of the author except as provided by USA copyright law.

The opinions expressed by the author are not necessarily those of Revival Waves of Glory Books & Publishing.

Published by Revival Waves of Glory Books & Publishing

PO Box 596 | Litchfield, Illinois 62056 USA

www.revivalwavesofgloryministries.com

Revival Waves of Glory Books & Publishing is committed to excellence in the publishing industry.

Book design Copyright © 2017 by Revival Waves of Glory Books & Publishing. All rights reserved.

Published in the United States of America

Paperback: 978-1-68411-217-3

Introduction

Fear is one of the daring enemies of yours that has vowed to limit your contribution to your generation. The spirit of fear loves to steal the will of man, to control it toward it pleasures, which results in men's passivity, immobility and lack of creativity. The right hand of the devil is fear, which means Satan himself is immobilized until the spirit of fear paves a way for him.

Hence, to conquer the enemy at the centre of your world, you need to conquer your fears.

Every kind of fear is destructive, it has torments, it has innate ability to disorganize and destabilize men's thoughts. The end time will be full of different occurrences that will hold many spell bound and shake the faith of many, but in the midst of these, God expects His children to stand firm because they have a special standing with Him.

"Men's heart failing them from fear and for looking after those things which are coming on the earth, for the powers of heavens shall be shaken." (Luke 21:26)

There is no fear in God, so in this end time, He expects His children to be bold and to be gloriously daring, so as to be able to use them to save many people from the jaws of lions and from the lion's den.

He never expects His children to be amidst end time victims but among end time victors, because end time days is simply not a good time for the unbelievers, but it will serve as glorious days for all God's children, who are not living with pride (not by sight) but are humbling living by faith.

"When men are cast down then thou shall say there is a lifting up and He shall save the humble person." (Job 22:29)

The end time is a time to explain your faith away or to start weeping like those that has no hope. It is not a time for us to be crawling into holes, dogging our head from enemies' darts because we are placed in the front to confront.

It is our prophetic time to arise and break the barricade of fear and pull down the walls of intimidations, militating against our heavenly mandates.

"But the people that do know their God shall be strong, and do exploits." (Daniel 11:32)

In this end time God is counting on you, tear that garment of fear off your heart and put on the new garment of faith for it is time to exploit with your God and for your God.

Shalom.

Contents

Introduction iii
Contents v
Chapter 1: What Is Fear 1
Chapter 2: Fear And The Christian.. 5
Chapter 3: There Is A Reason For All Fear 9
Chapter 4: Three Kinds Of Fear 12
Chapter 5: Way Out Of Fear...17
Chapter 6: Lessons From The Leviathan 20
Chapter 7: Fear Not, You Can't Be Caged...............................24
Chapter 8: Do You Know That You Can Decree Your Way Out Of Every Intimidating Situation? 29
Chapter 9: Fear Not, You Are A Pacesetter! 35
Chapter 10: The Fear Of Death...38
Chapter 11: Stand And Become A Standard 44
Chapter 12: Pratical Steps To Deal With The Spirit Of Fear 49
Chapter 13: You Are A Divine Sign..55
Chapter 14: Fear Not, You Have A Better Standing 58
Chapter 15: War Against the Spirit of Fear 64
Give Your Life To Christ Now!..73
Great Invitation 75

Chapter 1

WHAT IS FEAR

According to Oxford Advanced Learners Dictionary, fear is stated "as the bad feeling that you have when you are in danger, when you imagine that something bad might happen or when a particular thing frightens you, like the fear of the dark, spiders, and flight or flying objects. It is also stated as the act of avoiding danger or something unexpected.

Fear is 'false expectations arranged by your robbers". Satan is a globally accepted chief thief and one of his greatest devices is fear.

Fear is a spirit. It is a unique force in the hand of Lucifer against men of all ages, which means to have grown up to experience fear in your mind in respect of any issue, is to have encountered the greatest warlords at the centre of the world, the Devil himself.

The right hand of the devil is fear, it seems, and Satan cannot kill, maim, steal or destroy without fear at the centre. Anywhere Satan goes, fear paves ways, and it is the foremost foundation for many troubles, wars, heartaches and different demonic hardships in the world.

Segun T. Obadimu

Many wars, genocides, divorce, drug addictions, rebellions, confrontations, killings, destruction of all kinds have been solely found to be enshrined on fear of men. The more people keep increasing on the earth, the more hell comes against them with diverse tricks, crafts and other several attacks which leave men and women with utter perplexity.

FEAR THE GREATEST ENEMY OF MAN

On pages 13 and 69 of Global Population Trends, Warren C. Robins stated that in 1800 there were one million people in the world. In 1930, there were one billion people in the world. Thirty years later, in 1960, it was up to three billion. Fifteen years later, in 1975, four billion. Twelve years later, in 1987, it was five billion. Eleven more years in 1998, it was up to six billion. Sixteen years later, in 2014, it is now up to 7 billion.

But how many of these are being killed through fear daily? It seems to be the more mankind grows the merrier for his enemy to manipulate and destroy through cunning tricks and deception.

Global food production can no longer keep up with the exploding population. They try to control this by using chemical fertilizer, but due to the fear of the adverse effect on soil and men's health, through cancer, kidney problems and the rest this has to be reduced to the barest minimum.

Fear is the greatest world enemy besides Satan. It had been established that every natural man is with two traits, which can be either fear or anger but the truth is even anger itself is a product of fear and thought of insecurity.

WHAT FEAR HAS DONE TO OUR WORLD

FEAR NOT

We live in the midst of a chain reaction not only of technology, but also of evil; more crimes, more prisons, more misery, more diseases, more toxic wastes, worse food, worse air, worse drinking water, worse pollution, shootings, vandalism, land mines, terrorism, kidnaping and genocide.

It seems that everything good is also being used for everything bad. Consider the telephone, though it is helpful to the rest of us, yet it is used by drug lords to conduct business crime from prisons, and prostitution services are being run daily through cell phones from all our college dormitories. Hardly will you see any of our youth and adult alike who is not carrying mobile phones with pornographic pictures and videos, even the internet and e-mail is being overwhelmed by evil forces.

Today, every move made by a nation and her counterparts is seen as a threat to security.

On page 58 in his World Affairs Journal, Harry Ohen says: *From A.D 1500 to the present, the amount of potential power accessible at a single explosive detonation of a substance has increased ten billon times. "The destructive capacity of weaponry has been increasing exponentially throughout this century. Quite simply, humans are capable of killing other humans in greater numbers and more than ever before."*

It was even said that China, Iran, Iraq, North Korea, Syria, Sudan and Russia are all planning things world leaders are worried about, as the intelligent experts reveal that Russia is selling sensitive technology to several nations' intent on amassing weapons.

Today, the raw material of terrorist which is uranium or plutonium, which is been used to prepare either nuclear or 'dirty' (radioactive) bombs and what is called an explosive electronic device, can easily be obtained through the black market and numerous filthy means. All African countries, including my own beloved country (Nigeria), are living at the mercy of their own people for fear of the unknown exponentially throughout this century.

Chapter 2

FEAR AND THE CHRISTIAN

Christians are the foremost enemy of the power of fear, but which he cannot truly dominate and manipulate, because of the light of the Word that is embedded in their heart. He has not received the spirit of the world, which the devil can manipulate, in fact, he will need to go extra miles to dispatch another kind of spirit to confuse, distract and disturb their mind through unbelief. A true child of God has received a spirit that created the world itself. He has been endowed with power, wisdom and a graceful mind, the type of combination of force which is inside God who created the devil himself.

"For God has not given us the spirit of FEAR, but of power, and of love, and of a sound mind." (1 Timothy 1:7)

WHICH SPIRIT DID YOU RECEIVE?

If you are still afraid of the dark, or of the devil or the sea or your future, then which spirit did you receive?

Many fears are men, and what they can do to them, even that, at the expense of God, this is an error! Every kind of fear is destructive, it has torment, it has innate ability to disorganize and destabilize man's thoughts and divine plans. A housewife, due to fear after stealing some tokens from her wicked husband refused to tell him till she went to be with Lord. This single act was what brought her down to hell despite the fact that she did not use any of the money for her private use.

Fear of any kind comes from the bottom of hell; it is a spot in the life of a Christian. No matter the news or information you hear as a Christian, never allow it to move your heart away from Him, because anything that has a capacity to move your heart away from God has already succeeded in taking your soul to hell. Be determined to be brave for your God.

"But the FEARFUL, and unbelieving, and the abominable and murderers, and whore mongers and sorcerers and idolatries and liars shall have their part in the lake which burneth with fire and brimstone, which is the second death." (Rev. 21:7)

HOW DOES FEAR OPERATE?

It constantly put men and women under negative fires, tension and pressures to seek an alternative solution for their trouble. Satan is fear personified. He knows he is constantly living at the mercy of God, that he can be destroyed at any time, which is the same thought he is trying to share with you. How can God destroy the apple of His eye (i.e. you) suddenly? How can He handle you any how and treat you without mercy? But due to Satan's deception and lack of trust in God, many have been brought into the lies of the devil, and this has made them to fall out of grace with God. Remember, all of us leave out what we believe. If you believe that you will never make it or you will die prematurely, there is nothing God will do against it, it will come to pass, that is why the normal word of Christ to people is "let it be unto you according to your faith".

On page 8 in her book, Defeated Enemies, Corrie T. Boom, shares a story of some victims of German war which goes: "After the war in Germany there was among many people, great uncertainty about the soldiers that were missing. Were they still in Russian concentration camps or had they died fighting during the war? This uncertainty caused great suffering among their relatives and many people went to fortunetellers, to find out about their loved ones". After this step, he said later, "Many came to me and told me about permanent darkness in their heart and an urge to commit suicide".

Whenever the devil wants to capture a man to destroy him, he will send him into a state of confusion. He may send him into a state of uncertainty, a state in which his rest is totally under siege or under arrest.

Have you ever seen a man who sees himself clearly in troubled water? That is exactly the state of a man who is confused. God is not an author of confusion.

"For God is not the author of confusion, but of peace." (1Cor. 14:33).

After seeing that you have welcomed the news of confusion and uncertainty that he has brought your way, then he will begin to send his own vessels with his words to you (he might use somebody close to you) who will be telling you to seek a medium, a sorcerer, a fortuneteller, a white garment prophet or a prayer merchant the moment you yield to this, another powerful spirit will gain entrance into you, which work is to lead you to total destruction.

"There shall not find among you any one that maketh his son or his daughter to pass through the fire, or that useth divination, or an observer of times, or an enchanter or a witch or a charmer or

consulter with familiar spirit, or a wizard or a necromancer unto the Lord...thou shall be perfect with the Lord thy God." (Deut. 18:10-13)

Chapter 3

THERE IS A REASON FOR ALL FEAR

After seeing that you have welcomed the news of confusion and uncertainty that he has brought your way, then he will begin to send his own vessels with his words to you (he might use somebody close to you) who will be telling you to seek a medium, a sorcerer, a fortuneteller, a white garment prophet or a prayer merchant the moment you yield to this, another powerful spirit will gain entrance into you, which work is to lead you to total destruction.

"There shall not find among you any one that maketh his son or his daughter to pass through the fire, or that useth divination, or an observer of times, or an enchanter or a witch or a charmer or consulter with familiar spirit, or a wizard or a necromancer unto the Lord...thou shall be perfect with the Lord thy God." (Deut. 18:10-13)

As there is no smoke without a fire, so there is no fear without a reason. It comes for one major purpose, to break your fellowship with your greatest lover, your Lord.

A man that is in constant fear has been taken away from the presence of God; fear is lack of total assurance of victory of Christ over every world problem. Satan knows much about God's provision, and His abundant mercy more than men of all ages and he also knows that to access it you need to come to God's presence with clarity and precision of whom you are and your understanding of what Christ has made you to be before Him.

"Let us therefore come boldly unto the throne of grace that we may obtain mercy, and find grace to help in time of need. (Heb. 4:16)

DO NOT FEAR, HE IS YOUR "GUARDIAN" ANGEL

Fear tarries in the absence of faith, but it is neutralized in the presence of it. Faith is common currency that has innate ability to destroy fear to the root, but as common as it is, it is highly expensive for the world to access, except few, who have gotten their life washed by the blood of the Lamb. (Rev. 21:7)

I once had an experience with fear some years ago. (It is good to state here that there are common fears, which all men have, like hearing shocking news, and there are uncommon or extraordinary fears brought about by Satan through a situation).

Then, I was in a shift work in which my partner and I had to resume work in the evening and leave in the morning. It was a big company but surrounded with bush though there was a fence with night guards at the gate, yet, there was apprehension that robbers could come in the midnight to rob us and perhaps maim or kill us.

Anytime I was on duty, my brain would be calculating, and in those days power could be taken at any time (though not as incessant as it is today). So, we needed to rush out to switch on the big generator outside. Who knows if somebody has been waiting for this time to strike? I always thought in my heart. This had been the state of my heart till one day; the Lord spoke to my heart and said, "Fear not! You have an angel watching over you," and my eyes were open and I saw a tall man with suspended legs in the air with a sword in his right hand and blazing eyes like fire. Immediately, I became afraid but the Lord assured me again saying, "Do not fear for he is your guardian angel." From that day till I left that company, I never harbored any fear, because I know my angel is always in charge as written in His word.

"For He shall give his angels charge over thee." (Psalm 91:11)

GET RID OF SECRET SIN

Fears tarry when you do not find out your worth in the Word and believe it. It tarries if you are still harboring secret sins in your life.

Stolen waters are sweet, and bread eaten in secret is pleasant. But he knoweth not that the dead are there and that her guests are in the depth of hell. (Prov. 9:17)

If you are still a liar, a fornicator, a backbiter, a gossiper, idol worshiper or still seek white garment churches, herbalist, fake prophets, then you are still within its arms. Sit down, today and do a holistic check of your walk with your God and screen your life journey till date. Is there any time in which you have toiled with the enemy; directly or indirectly? Even if you follow somebody to an herbalist or a sorcerer, there is an adage, that says, "He that does not want water to wet his cloth will not follow any one to the river side."

There is no way you will have contact with demonic men and women with their materials without having their spirit hang around you.

Chapter 4

THREE KINDS OF FEAR

There are three kinds of fear; the first one is the fear of man to man, the second is the fear of the Devil while the third is the fear of God.

FEAR OF MAN

Jesus Christ warns us seriously against this as it can lead us to eternal destruction.

"And fear not them which kill the body, but are not able to kill the soul, but rather fear Him which is able to destroy both soul and the body in hell." (Mathew10:28)

This is a common fear that many in the world possess. It has made many to compromise the gospel of Christ (Matthew 10:32) and shy away from their spiritual responsibility to many people around them.

A boy became born again and was highly persecuted by his father, who was a Muslim, and other family members. Later due to pressure and intimidation by his father and others, he succumbed to their wishes; he backslides and began to follow them to the mosques. After a few months, he died. Months later, the father became born again and they asked the father, "Why did you persecute your son to that extent, since you know he is on the right way? He answered and said, "It was my boy who did not know whom he had received. After all, he knew I was only acting in ignorance."

Who is that man you are afraid of at the expense of God? Drop that fear before it leads you to hell. (Rev. 21:7)

FEAR OF THE DEVIL

Sometime ago, my wife and I were coming from a trip. We were in a bus, when suddenly one fetish man stood up and began to make strong incantation, and later introduced himself as the head of all wizards and openly challenged any witch in the bus to dare his power. After this, everywhere was totally plunged into silence and fear gripped everybody except yours sincerely and his wife. Immediately, he sprang into action and began to sell his traditional medicine and everybody in the bus began to demand for it like hot cakes.

Suddenly, I felt so annoyed within me at this agent of the devil and I stood up, and said, "Sir, if you are looking for money for food, why don't you ask us for a donation and we would have done so with all our hearts? Why do you have to plunge people's lives into slavery all in the name of business?" And I looked at those people that had bought his demonic drugs and I made a decree, neutralizing it in their hands and I described my name and my church denomination and called my number three times that if what they had in their hands would ever work they should call me on my cell phone.

Fear of Satan begins from fearing the dark, and thinking something is there secretly to harm you. Many cannot go near water, streams or rivers. Many cannot kill ordinary fowl. Others are being threatened daily by spiders, dogs, birds, rats, cockroaches and wall geckos. Many are afraid of the night for no just cause. These kind of people sense evil in all things and they are too chicken hearted that they will mostly think with their legs, all the time, instead of them confronting their fears head long they bow out in frustration. Even many servants of the Lord who should be at the fore-front campaigning against Satan and demonic powers are the first to dodge deliverance cases despite the promise made available in His word.

"And these signs shall follow them that believe; in my Name shall they cast out devils." (Mark 16:17)

WHO ARE YOU?

One day, the Holy Ghost revealed to me a young lady who has a big snake curled around her to her neck. This is her spiritual power! As many that have anything to do with her, will automatically be initiated into the marine world. That day, I called her and as we were discussing, suddenly I asked with holy anger, "Who are you?"

Suddenly her face changed, and her looks became like that of a monster and she uttered the cruelest and intimidating word I have never heard before in my life. "You are too small, go and call your pastor?" (She mentioned the name of the pastor).

Immediately I looked up and said, "Father, I thank you because you always answer my prayers."

Immediately after I said that she burst into weeping, and she began to confess that she had killed many people, she had caused many accidents…"Please, please, Brother Segun, help me."

If I had not known whom I had believed, I would have received more than I bargained for on that day.

FEAR NOT

The truth here is, it takes Satan to produce a satanic manifestation.

Satan is all fears, manifesting fears in your life or living it, which simply means you need deliverance through the word. God does not manifest fear and His word does not either. Fear is from the pit of hell, while His word is light. His word cannot be living in you and you will still be full of fear.

I am the light of the world; he that followeth me shall not walk in darkness, but shall have the lights of life. (John 8:12)

Fear in you simply means you lack much light (the word) in you. Several years ago, we went to Ado-Ekiti to start a branch of our church. The premises we were using for a church was adjourned with a residential house. The residents of this house are idol worshipers with the shrine of their god in the passage of their house. The name of this god was "Imole" (the god of light.) One day, I went secretly to the shrine which was covered with a white cloth, I lifted the cloth up and saw different things they were using to worship this idol and I picked one of the items (a local gong) and brought it down to the church. The moment some of our members saw it with me, they fled from me saying, "That's exactly the god the people always come to worship even from other states." I later dropped it into the dustbin; this made them to believe in the true God.

The Lord is my light and my salvation, whom shall I fear? The Lord is the strength of my life of whom shall I be afraid? (Psalm 27:1)

I FOUND A CHRISTMAS GIFT

Another day, I was going to the house when I saw a big bowl of salt at the junction that led to our house. I wondered why it must be wasted when we did not have enough salt for cooking at home. I waited till night and brought a nylon and packed it so as to use it at home. Since it was a festival period, I gave some to our neighbor as a Christmas gift, and they all returned their gestures with much appreciation. God never told his children to ignore Satan and his powers, but He never told them to fear him.

There is nothing to fear about Satan and his agents, for the tallest of them ends at the bottom of your feet. You are not only a heir of Christ (Gal. 4:1) you are also made complete in Him who is the head of all principalities and power. (Col. 2:10)

GODLY FEAR

"And the fear of the Lord fell on the people, and they came out with one consent." (1 Sam. 11:7)

This is the only fear recommended by God to his children. This type of fear is endorsed by divinity to be seen or found in all men. Wisdom is the chief cornerstone through which a man builds his house and the only way described as gaining an access to it is through the fear of the Lord.

"The fear of the Lord is beginning of wisdom." (Psalm 111:10)

You can't prevail over the devil until this is put perfectly in place in your soul. You can only resist, rebuke and bind enemies through the wisdom of God, hence, you need to walk in His ways, obey His statutes and fear Him above all things, and then all lesser fears will naturally recede.

Chapter 5

WAY OUT OF FEAR

"*There is no fear in love but perfect love casteth out fear.*" *(1 John 4:18)*

The way out of all your fears is to walk in love, pure love is the pillar behind all boldness of men, and you must constantly exercise your conscience to be void of all offences before God and before men.

"And here I do exercise myself, to have always a conscience void of offence towards God and towards men." (Acts 24:16)

Many hearts are full with offences; they find it difficult to walk in peace with those who have opposite views from theirs. Some are fire brands in their neighborhood while some bosses and political leaders have used veto power and political "wheel" to "will" many goods to themselves through diverse deceptive means. Such people are wicked and cannot or never have peace. A husband that refuses to love his wife despite her humility and total obedience will always live in constant fear of the unknown, and the same thing goes to a wife that does not love her husband enough as to be in total subjection to him. A fraudster and an embezzler are all not living in peace with their neighbors. They can never be free from fear. Why do prominent people die of cardiac arrest? It is mostly because contrary to what people know, their hearts have been surrounded and engrossed with evil that with a slight shaking, he or she will quickly think maybe his numerous 'shady deals' have been uncovered. Hence, what does the Bible say, "Owe no man nothing except love."(Roman 13:8) Don't owe money, don't owe promise, do not exercise yourself on high things. If you are still at the base today, remain there in the process of time, and with prayer, God will turn the tides, for there is never a true success without a due process.

Do not go out of the way of God to be rich.

One day, a man with fear came to see a pastor after a Sunday service to confess how he had gotten a lot of money through rituals. However, he was pleading that he did not need such money again and that the Pastor should follow him home to destroy the power because he wanted to be free so as to serve God.

My dear, to come out from evil nets may not be as easy as you think. So be determined to walk in love from today, and patiently and with contentment begin to live your life to please heaven so with time your change will come and Heaven will speak. "Thou shall arise, and have mercy upon Zion, for the time to favour her, yea the set time is come." (Ps. 102:13) It is my prayer as you patiently wait upon the Lord, your set time will come and you will laugh last, in Jesus name, Amen.

SECTION A

FEAR YOUR GREATEST ENEMY OF ALL TIME

Chapter 6

LESSONS FROM THE LEVIATHAN

It had been said that there are about thirty thousand promises of God for man in His word. While A.W Tozer said, "A promise is as good as the character of him who said it," the words 'fear not' are everywhere in the word of God. Some people even said it appears 365 times which means that it is 'fear not' for each day. God had a preknowledge of the kind of a burden fear will connote for mankind so God gave Job an analysis of an animal called 'Leviathan'. I want you to learn something from it as you follow me in this book.

YOU CANNOT BE TRAPPED BY YOUR TONGUE EXCEPT YOU WILL

"Can't thou draw out Leviathan with a hook or his tongue with a cord thou lettest down?" (Job 41:1)

A crocodile does not open its mouth anyhow like a fish except whenever it wants to eat.

FEAR NOT

Have you said anything wrong somewhere that made you panic, because saying it may be used against you? Stand up now and erase it with the blood of Jesus and take a step to right the wrong (Prov. 6:2-3). Remember no fish can be hooked until it opens its mouth in the water. So are you always using your tongue wisely, for your tongue is a blessing.

YOU ARE NOT DESIGNED TO MAKE AN ENTREATMENT WITH YOUR ENEMY

"Will he make many supplications unto thee? Will he speak soft words unto thee. Will he make a covenant with thee? Will thou take him for a servant forever"? (Job41:3-4)

Leviathan does not beg its enemy neither does it retreat or surrender because it believes in the grace God has given to conquer all battles.

For many of us the moment we find ourselves in the form of a man (with some suffering, under some negative tendencies) instead of humbling ourselves just like Christ did (Phil. 2:8), we begin to look for an easy way out, or look for a short cut. You cannot have a lion share until you have a lion's heart. You must be bold enough to face every challenge that comes your way, just as Christ did on His way to the cross. On your way to your cross, don't chicken out, don't supplicate, don't give soft words or make a covenant (bribery) for your release, let Him have His ways, and fear not, you will laugh last.

FEAR SHOULD NOT MAKE YOU LOSE YOUR HONOUR

"Will thou play with him as with a bird? Or will thou bind him for thy maidens?" (Job 41:5)

One of the fascinating things about this animal is that it can hardly be used as a toy or pet in the hand of anyone.

Many today, through fear have become the opposite of their true self. They have allowed un-favourable cases and circumstances which naturally would have taken with old story.

How can you allow trouble to tie you down when you have the wing to fly?

When you have the Holy Ghost, you are too big and too loaded spiritually and potentially to be used as a toy in the hands of anybody. Arise today and begin to lose your wings in tongues to God, for it is time to fly higher.

You Are Not Designed To Be A Prey Or A Source Of Food

TO PRAYER CONTRACTORS OR PRAYER MERCHANTS.

"Shall the companions make a banquet of him? Shall they part him among the merchants?" (Job 41:6)

Recently, I was looking for a way described for me but when I couldn't get it I saw a well-dressed man and I approached him to show me the way. He gladly did and later, after we had discussed for a while, he said, "I do pray for people that is my job. If you need my service please contact me through my number." I received his number but laughed at him in my mind. Many of us, due to fear of the unknown, uncertainty and unbelief, have been making mere prayer contractors to make merchandise of us.

A professor went to a herbalist for power. He gave him a date when he would come back for it, On the D-day; he left for the herbalist's home in the morning. Upon getting there, he met his younger son whom he had given a message that anytime the professor came he should give him the concoction under the bed. Unknowingly to the boy, he carried the 'pottee' in which the herbalist had, the professor took it and went away. The third day, with gladness of heart, the professor came back to appreciate the herbalist for the job well done, and behold, he met the herbalist in a sad state. What happened sir? I just came to appreciate you on the good job you had done. "The charm really worked." The herbalist looked at him and told him exactly what happened and the rest of the story might well be guessed.

Another man went back to his herbalist a day before the due date. He did not only meet the herbalist having a nice time with the 'good chicken' which he donated, he also saw the herbalist's wife wearing the lace materials he bought for his rituals.

Do not allow your lack of faith and unbelief to make lesser of a man to banquet on your predicament. Sow your money, your service and your time to God on behalf of that case. God is a rewarder of those that diligently seek Him, and He will reward you accordingly.

Chapter 7

FEAR NOT, YOU CAN'T BE CAGED

"*Can't thou fill his skin with barbed irons or his head with fish spears*"? *(Job 41:7)*

Any other destiny may be caged with spiritual barbed iron, the satanic weapons may have succeeded in drilling out the divine visions out of their head, but as far as you are concerned, fear not, as such a thing like this will not happen to you. Not only will He prevent you from all kinds of bondage from any realm, He will also see to it that no weapon formed against you will prosper, be it spiritual or temporal!

Your destiny cannot or can never be under siege, for you are a seed of God, a seed of a winner, a seed of a champion, and you can never be destroyed.

TO TOUCH YOU IS TO TOUCH THE APPLE OF HIS EYE

"Lay thine hands on him; remember that battle, do it no more." (Job 41:8)

Do you know that you are a special breed to God? Do you know that you are unique and peculiar to heaven? Do you know that heaven relies more on you to do wonders in the world through his Holy Spirit? Some years ago, a friend of mine went to preach somewhere, suddenly one cultic man came out from their lodge with a Dane gun, shot sporadically in the air three times, and brought out an amulet with charm, rushed towards him and beat him three times saying, "I give you seven days." At the end of the seventh day, my friend went back to the front of the same lodge to raise his voice for God. Immediately, the man saw him, fear and shame covered him like a garment and he began to run away. Immediately, those who witnessed the scenario seven days ago began to run after him calling him all manners of names.

Beloved, cheer up, you are untouchable, you are indestructible and you are unconquerable the list is endless.

Sometime ago, an un-believer took the money I gave him to repair something for me and absconded with it. After some time, he came back telling me, that on that very day, God miraculously saved him from an accident that would have taken his life! He also said that since that time he had desired my prayer and forgiveness.

I forgave him and prayed with him, giving him the money. God knows how to recompense tribulation to those that trouble you. If those that try to hurt a common leviathan in the water, cannot go without a wound, how much more will those that trouble you?

Some years ago, there was this woman who was highly elevated but never saw anything good coming out of me, so we daily related like Mordecai and Haman (Esther 3:1-8) because I know that I have a glorious future so I decided to face my life and my God.

One day, a call was made for us to go and pray for one dying woman in the hospital. Lo and behold, it was this woman! Our eyes met during the prayers but then she could not talk any longer. Alas she died the second day.

"Seeing it is righteous thing with God to recompense tribulation to them that trouble you." (2 Thessalonians 1:6)

THE STRENGTH WITH YOU IS MORE THAN THE ONE WITH YOUR ENEMY

"Behold, the hope of him is in vain, shall not one be cast down even at the sight of him?"– (Job 41:9)

None is so fierce that dares stir him up. You cannot engage a crocodile in battle like any other creatures because of his tail which is structured like sharp blade, or its body which is full of thick scales, or his mouth which is full of poisonous teeth and because of his sharp claws.

Years ago, a mother invited us to pray for her daughter. We were about to start when the Lord suddenly directed me to pray only for her daughter and leave the mother alone. Within a few seconds into the prayer the daughter began to shout, saying, "She, she, she," pointing to her mother because she was the one behind her troubles. The problem started when the mother decided to donate her as a successor in her coffin but she refused vehemently because of her belief. I later prayed with her and with the help of the Holy Ghost, the spirit was cast out of her.

Due to this, the mother marked me down telling all ears that cared to listen that I connived with her daughter to call her a witch.

One day, I met her on my way and greeted her. Immediately, right there on the road, she began to threaten me with big swelling words that had to do with her position in their mystical world. Suddenly, a holy anger rose up from within me and I directed my finger at her and said, "Ma, you may be old enough to give birth naturally to me but spiritually you are a little baby."

This further infuriated her and influenced her to do more evil against me. But when she saw that my God was always with me (Jer. 20:14), she resulted into blackmailing and lying about me to many people. But I kept my silence.

Recently, her daughter called and said that she was sick and that she wanted me to help pray for her. I told her to help me do the job. Two weeks later, my wife came in from a birthday party, telling me that many of the participants were rushing to attend a funeral of an aged woman. Lo and behold, our dear mother had given up the ghost!

Do you ever think of the reason the enemy of your soul comes in the midnight, when you are fast asleep? Do you ever think of the reason he always creeps in to attack you, when you are un-aware? Do you ever think of the reason he needs to trick and deceive you before he can cage or attack you? It is because by divine standings, you are in command of authority and power rather than him. He cannot face you one on one because he cannot stand your full force. This will tell you the level of the power in the custody of your enemy compared to you.

GOD DOES NOT ONLY WANT YOU TO KNOW HIM, HE WANTS YOU TO BE PROUD OF HIM IN EVERY BATTLE

"His scales are his pride, shut up together as close seal, one is no near to another, that no air can come in between them....they stick together that they cannot be sundered." (Job 41:15-17)

Here the pride of this animal was divinely revealed, the glory that surrounds its body that could not allow its enemies to tame or destroy it are its scales. They were so close to each other that even the thin air cannot penetrate them or cut them asunder. Beloved, the Bible says that "He that glory, let him glory of the Lord." (1 Cor 1: 3)

When last have you appreciated the mystery of the trinity in your life? Do you know that no force on earth and in heaven can break the seal of the Holy Ghost around you? Do you know that the Trinity is fixed together that no manipulation, schemes or demonic crafts can cut through? Are you also aware that as Leviathan is surrounded with thick and close scales so are you enclosed within the power of the Holy Trinity? The greatest force on the earth is at your disposal. If the ordinary air cannot penetrate the scales of the common animal to reach his body, do you think even an extra ordinary air will penetrate the Trinity to reach you? Lift up your faith to Him, for you are more than secured.

Chapter 8

DO YOU KNOW THAT YOU CAN DECREE YOUR WAY OUT OF EVERY INTIMIDATING SITUATION?

"*By his sneezing a light doth shine...His breadth kindleth coals, and a flame goeth out of his mouth.*" *(Job 41:18-21)*

This is another mysterious thing about this animal. He knows what to do in the midst of darkness and that is to produce a light instead of throwing a pity party. He knows that to move forward, he only needs to look inward. He knows how to use every feature in his head to bring about a turnaround.

Being cowed, intimidated or being fearful has nothing to do with your problem. It only worsens it, because you stop decreasing when you start decreeing. The Word says, "You will decree a thing, it shall be established unto you, and light shall shine in your way." (Job 22:28) Like the animal we are highlighting here, everything you need to spark the fire is within your mouth. (Job 41:19)

A brother got married as an impotent man. Having prayed and received a go ahead from the Lord, he went ahead with the wedding. After the wedding proper, the brother went in with his wife in order to culminate the wedding. He checked his manhood, and it was still the same as before. He told his newly wedded bride to give him some time to clean himself up. On getting to the toilet, he naked himself and told God, "Lord, today, I know you cannot put me to shame, ah Lord! I know you cannot put me to shame!" He kept on repeating these words on and on and suddenly, the miracle happened. His manhood lifted up and he went in to his wife.

What he did might not seem like a decree, but it was a spiritual code that he needed to do from the bottom of his heart for the light to shine upon his ways. One day, several years ago, when I was staying with my unbelieving uncle, he brought a charm into the house for his personal use but I found it offensive due to my belief and declared that the charm will not work in his hand. He was so annoyed and told me to pack my belongings and leave his house. Since I had nowhere to go and had no money to rent a house of my own, I decreed that God should find another house for him. A few days later, to the day he gave to me to pack and get out, he came in and told me he had gotten another apartment for himself and that he would be leaving the room for me.

You too have all it takes, start now, and your light will shine.

YOU HAVE ALL IT TAKES TO FINE-TUNE YOUR INABILITY TO ABILITY

"In his neck remaineth strength, and sorrow is turned into joy before him." (Job 41:22)

Bravo! Even the animal knows how to turn weakness to strength, to turn inability to ability. If there is anything you must learn about God, you must learn to wait on Him until your change comes. (Job 14:14)

FEAR NOT

Challenges are common to man, but in the midst of challenges, despite that many eyes are looking only a few eyes can see the inherent grace such situations have come to offer them.

Do you know that until you suffer you cannot offer and until you begin to offer you cannot be preferred.

Learn today from this, your sorrow is there for God to fine tune. Every man in the Bible, including Christ and various great men, were one time people with one sorrow or the other, but they turned theirs to joy. You are the next in line for joy. Amen.

LET YOUR HEART BE FIXED

"His heart is as firm as a stone, yea, as hard as a piece of the nether millstone." (Job 14:24)

For the fact that your heart is fearful simply means your heart is not totally fixed on your God.

"Let thine eyes look right on and let thine eyelids look straight before thee." (Prov. 4:25)

An unstable heart is a fearful heart which cannot receive anything from the Lord. If God can cite an example of animal in respect of his heart and so much honor him that he puts his name and attribute into his eternal word so that His children can learn from him, how much more he will do for you, so as to use you as a case study for his children. With God there is nothing a fixed heart cannot fix. There is no phase he cannot succumb. Fix your gaze solely on Him and soon, you will begin to attract your needed grace from nooks and crannies of your world.

SEGUN T. OBADIMU

YOU ARE A MIGHTY MAN OF VALOUR

"When he raised up himself the mighty are afraid, by reason of breaking they purify themselves,.....He esteemeth iron as straw, brass as rotten wood. The arrow cannot make him flee....he laughed at the shaking of a spear." (Job 41:25-29)

Taking notes of all these revelations being revealed by God about this animal thus makes us to appreciate the grace He has given to man, most especially, the redeemed. We are awesome beings that have no reason to fail despite stiff opposition. God says here that whenever a Leviathan rises up himself for battle, the mighty are afraid. The question is when will you rise up to fight the battle of your life as a man? Fear and lack of vision had almost killed Gideon until he had an encounter with an angel who restored him back and called him what he really was which he was not really aware of (Judges 6:12) because he had been blindfolded by his foundational problem and the situation around him. "Hear ye now what the Lord saith; Arise, contend thou before the mountains, and let the hills hear thy voice."(Micah 6:1)

Most of Satan's tricks in our lives always move us to argue with the Word. Until we stop that and see our lives in the light of His Word, we can never see the battle of our lives as nothing.

The difference between man and the animal kingdoms is that while our kingdom is full of confusion because of unbelief and argument, the animal kingdom is daily enjoying expansion for taking God for whom He is and daily living the way He was designed, with total regard for hierarchy. If not for men's distraction, their population would have almost over shadowed the world of men.

Arrows of men should not make you panic. You don't need to regard an iron as far as your life is concerned, more than a straw, you don't need to be frightened at the shaking of a spear. If God says an animal laughs at it, how about you then? The battle of the world is the survival of the

FEAR NOT

fittest. It has to do more on your profession and divine perception of yourself. A clear perception of your worth will make you to laugh and rest in the midst of opposition.

Some years ago, a woman whom the Lord revealed to me to be a witch was trading words with me. She suddenly got angry and said, "If care is not taken, I will report you to my spiritual mothers and I give you seven (7) days, and you will become a history." And I looked at her and laughed and said, "You and your spiritual mothers are lazy and weak, even to kill a human being in an hospital does not take more than a second, just inject him with a poisonous needle and he is gone." After saying this, I looked at her face to face and said, "If you talk more arrogantly again in that manner, I will be provoked to call my Father in Heaven right here and you will become a dead person." Immediately after she heard this, she quietly came to my side and began to beg me. It is so surprising that even those of the kingdom of Satan know what we are capable of, but we know less than nothing of the great stuff we are made of. You are a mighty man of valor therefore don't die a coward.

GO FOR THE WORD

"Sharp stones are under him, he spreadeth sharp pointed things upon the mire......" (Job 41:30)

David did not go for the natural sword. He went out for the stones, the Spiritual Sword.

A 'mire' here stands for frustrating and difficult situations. The literal meaning stands for an area of deep mud which can mean a state of deep mess and shame but you don't need to fear the situation. The Bible says, "the word of God is quick, and powerful, sharper than any two edged sword." (Heb 4:12) Target your word, which is the sent sword against the mire, just like David did, but then, the Word of God has to be dwelling in you richly with all wisdom. The word says; "sharp stones are under him," not one stone, not just one scripture but a myriad of them. Go for the word and I see your world turning into a heavenly bliss.

Chapter 9

FEAR NOT, YOU ARE A PACESETTER!

"*He maketh the sea like a pot of ointment; He maketh a path to shine after Him....*" *(Job 41:31-32)*

He is a pathfinder, he levelled up valley for the people to tour, he brings down the difficult mountain for men behind him to tread softly, and he is a pacesetter. He with his divine energy turns pace to grace. There are difficult things people cannot afford to do because they could not access them, so they become a problem, a sea of trouble, but through his fearless spirit, he can weather the storm, create a path, a channel for men, in between the sea. Even after he has long gone, the path he has created still remains as visible as ever and the light he had ignited is still shining for coming generation to embrace. Hence, remember, the greater the head the greater the headache.

Do not let your fear cripple you and your potentials, you are not only essential for the contemporary world but also designed to be a great blessing for the coming generation.

LIVING IN FEAR IS LIVING IN THE SHADOW OF YOURSELF

Segun T. Obadimu

"Upon earth there is not his like who is made without fear."(Job 41:33)

You are created in the beginning without fear; you are in the cast of Lion who turneth not away for any in battle (Prov. 30:30) that is why you are a breed of the Lion of the tribe of Judah.

Stop living in the shadow of God's mind for your life, take charge, take control, stay in the position God has given you.

"Cast not away therefore your confidence, which hath great recompense of reward, for ye have need of patience, that after ye have done the will of God, ye might receive the promise." (Heb. 10:35-36)

YOU ARE BORN TO TALK TOUGH

"He beholdeth all high things; he is a king over all the children of pride." (Job 41: 34)

Remember that if your mind is fashioned like that of mosquito you will still be misquoted, how much more having the mind of Christ? (Phil. 2:5)

You cannot have the heart of God and not be misquoted.

One of the chief traits of a man with a fearless spirit is that he believes that there is nothing His God cannot do, no matter how great. The more the difficulty of the situation, the more he talks tough. When people see small and shallow things, their eyes are on great and big things. When the king of Israel was being intimidated by Goliath, David, a little boy, an un-trained and unqualified soldier was seeing high things. He so much exercised his faith in whom he believed that he incurred the wrath of his brothers.

"And Eliab his eldest brother heard when he spake unto the men and Eliab's anger was kindled against David and he said, why

comest down hither? And with whom hast thou left those few sheep in the wilderness? I know thy PRIDE, and the naughtiness of thine heart. For thou art come down that thou mightiest see the battle." (1 Sam. 17:28)

The chosen few are the fearless ones, who daily take pride in their God. He is called the 'king' because his pride is distinctively divine. His peculiar pride does not cause commotion but a divine contribution which aids men and women out of their gallows and shame. When other types of pride will kill an ant and be asking men to honor them, his own type of pride will kill a giant (Goliath) and immediately endeared men's hearts to themselves. His own pride is based on total conviction of the ability of God.

When others take pride in their earthly achievement and in who they are in the eyes of men, he boldly takes pride in whom he is in God and in his awesome power.

"That according as it is written, He that glorieth, let him glory in the Lord." (1 Cor. 1:31)

Having seen all the traits highlighted by God concerning you, using a mere animal as an example, the creature which is compared to your skills, intelligent quotient, wisdom, grace and candor are a lot lower to your standard. What next? Will you still continue daily living like a tortoise and snail that are too slow in their journey?

Chapter 10

THE FEAR OF DEATH

A great woman of God, Maria Beula Woodworth Etter, was always facing life threatening confrontations from wicked people around where God had sent her to evangelize. Anytime she prepared to start her crusade, some people who come from nowhere would gain their entrance into the people to distract and cause commotion. She said one day; "I had been in great dangers, many times, not knowing when I would be shot down, either on the pulpit or going to and fro from meetings. But I said I would never run nor compromise. The Lord would always put His mighty power on me, so that He took all fears away, and made me like a giant… If anyone has tried to shoot or kill me, HE would strike them dead, and I sometimes tell them so." This great woman died at the age of eighty.

The mother of all fears is the fear of death, the fear of death is a great misery that the world would love to spend all their fortune to un-ravel.

They have tried all means within their frames to understand it and it is so apparent that it is beyond their spheres. It towers high, well beyond the realm of their understanding.

Scientists have tried to proffer solutions but they all meet with delusion and confusion.

It was even funny that a medical practitioner, who headed a committee to research on life saving initiatives, recently, slumped and died suddenly before the research was carried out.

Satan even came up with "Judas therapy" (suicide) to help all men and women who want to save face from shame and difficult situations. He will say, "What is there again on the earth for you, kill yourself and escape this stressful world to enter the rest waiting for you in heaven!" Many have left the world with this thought but I'm sure their bodies will be rotting in hell.

It has been said that the moment a man discovers that he is left with no hope; he heads straight away to commit suicide.

Sometime ago, a man left his family, got to the main bridge which had the sea underneath, jumped headfirst into it and died. People who saw him thought he was just having a sight-seeing only to discover later that he actually went there to commit suicide.

Recently during the latest economic depression that engulfed the world through the stock exchange market, a man who had five children, three boys and two girls, called his wife one day signaling to her that they had to find a way of escaping the imminent shame that was coming upon them. He told her to go into a room with her two daughters and 'take care of them' and that he would do likewise with the three boys. By the second day, they could not but groan in tears as they had to carry all the seven bodies out of the room one by one. The two parents had murdered their five children and in turn 'taken care of themselves'.

Another fear of death that has ravaged the world at large is the menace of religious fanaticism.

It was Blaise Pascal who said, "Men never do evil so completely and cheerfully as when they do it from religious conviction."

It is the militant children of Ishmael Islam that is the biggest threat. Mohammed taught his followers that when one of his followers dies in battle against the infidels, he will instantly go to heaven and be forever waited on by seventy-two virgins who will feed and provide for his every comfort. Hence every day, additional suicide volunteers offer their services to carry out any mission assigned to them against Israel, the "great Satan" (an Iranian nick name for America) or any other place they are told to go.

These vain teachings for a deceptive reward have really cushioned their confidence to carry out the act of terrorism. This and other personal threats to life has really made the life of an ordinary being cumbersome.

"Men hearts failing them for fear, and for looking after those things which are coming on the earth…." (Luke 21:26)

"But you are not like the men God is talking about here, you are his special sons and daughters, you are His end time army and His saint of inestimable value, you are not to fear what they fear because your rock is not their rock, so your fate cannot be their fate."

However, to us death is not a catastrophe; it is a divine appointment, a divine entrance to our glorious rest. We have control over every form of death because its power is in the hand of our love and saviour who conquer it and gain victory over it.

"He shall enter into peace; they shall rest in their beds, each one walking in his righteousness." (Isa: 57:2)

"For death has been swallowed up in victory and the victory o death where is thy sting? O grave, where is thy victory?" (1 Cor. 15:54-55)

To us death happens in his time by the permission of our Lord not by the manipulation of any god for He knows our month and our years have been divinely stated by Him, which no god of the earth can truncate.

"Seeing his days are determined, the number of his months is with thee, thou hast appointed his bounds that he cannot pass." (Job 14:5)

It is an abomination for a Christian to be afraid of witches and wizards; it is a slap in the face of His God. It is likened to a son of a field marshal, a general or a president of a nation to be held hostage by a corporal for no just cause. Even if there is a cause, a word from his mouth is more than enough for him to break out from such hostage, not to talk of having his father's intervention.

SPIRIT OF DEATH ALWAYS COME WITH A MESSAGE.

The spirit of death comes with the fear of death. It will be telling you, 'You will die when travelling.' 'You will die while sleeping.' 'You will die of sicknesses. 'Your children will not grow up to old age.' 'You will not enjoy the fruits of your labour due to sudden death.' 'You will not live to your parent's age.' 'Armed robbers will break-in and kill you.' 'Try and commit suicide to escape this harsh world.' 'Witches in your family will kill you one day.' 'The enemy can kill you at any time.' The list is endless, and to believe anyone of these clearly shows that your heart is void of the knowledge of the word. It means that you are yet to be grounded and established in the Word of God.

MY ENCOUNTER WITH THE SPIRIT OF DEATH

Some years ago, I lost my father and it happened that before he died, he had been sick for many years and I had been around him for the space of eight years. During these years of his illness, he had stayed in my house for almost four and half years and eventually gave up the ghost in my house. Immediately after he died, I left my house for two weeks to refresh myself and also for a change of environment. I came back to the house only to see that I began to experience a new thing in my own room. The spirit of fear was too real that instantly it became uncomfortable to sleep on my bed. I would be hearing a voice saying, "You are the next to die." If I tried to sleep, I would be having demonic dreams and be pressed on the bed. I quoted every Bible passage I know, but it was like I was just talking to myself and any slight noise in the dead of the night caused me to become so frightened.

I knew that the devil wanted to use that situation to put me in bondage. I knew my dad to be a great lover, who loved all his children dearly and I know the scriptures well enough to know that the dead do not come back to the world.

GOD GAVE ME A WORD

One night I couldn't sleep and I decided to attend to a certain church night vigil which I was invited to but had decided against before. Throughout the night, till the morning my mind was on God, trying to be sensitive to hear the word He had to give me during this trying period.

All of a sudden, they called a sister to minister in song, and she quoted a scripture that was the end of my fear of death till date, she quoted Hebrew 2:14-15;

"Forasmuch then as the children are partakers of flesh and blood, he also himself likewise took part of the same that through death he might destroy him that hath the power of death, that is the devil; and deliver them who through fear of death were all their lifetime subject to bondage."

Whoa! Are you telling me that through the death of my lover, (He who loves me enough to lay down his life for me) the power of death has finally changed hands, which means the power to kill is now solely in the hand of Him who loves me, he that loves me cannot hurt me and if he does, it is for a greater gain, hence Paul says for me to die is gain.

"For to me to live is Christ and to die is gain." (Phil. 1:21)

I left the place in the morning with great understanding of who I am in God and the divine knowledge of what Christ has done for me. I discovered He actually did three things. He put on flesh like I am. He put himself in my place to help me. He chose to die in order to destroy him that held the power to kill me at will, without mercy, that part mostly comforted my soul and lastly, he gave you and I and every unborn generation a ticket endorsed by His blood, which states that anytime Satan and his agents threatens to kill us, we are to remind him of the death of the son of God, which means they will only succeed against us if Christ did not die at all.

Hence, so far as Satan cannot die and resurrect he has no power over life and death again, most especially on us who are believers.

"I am He that liveth, and was dead, and behold I am alive for evermore Amen, and have the keys of hell and of death." (Rev. 1:18)

In his book, Victorious Prayer, T.L. Osborn shared a story that goes:

"When General McArthur met the supreme commander of the Japanese forces at the end of World War II, he stripped the glistering medals from his chest, took the sword out of his hand and as the world watched; he declared total victory for the allies and enforced the term surrender."

This is what Christ has come to do for you on the cross. Your death is no longer in the hand of your enemy.

Chapter 11

STAND AND BECOME A STANDARD

"*Now the just shall live by faith; but if any man draws back, my soul shall have no pleasure in him.*" *(Heb. 10:38)*

It was Nelson Mandela of South Africa that said, "The only way to be brave is conquer your fear." Another man named Roosevelt said, "What we all need to fear is fear itself." Hence, Thomas Edison's fear of the dark was so great that it led him to invent a lightbulb.

Good destiny is one thing that the devil hates with a passion. He hates everything called glory with a perfect hatred. Greatness in life is not meant for the mediocre, it is a reserved dividend for the courageous.

God wants you to cause a slow motion by putting your grace into motion.

Fear is a major spirit that a child of destiny will need to overcome to achieve his God ordained mission. He must learn all it takes to fight the good fight of faith. The truth about all fear is that we still believe we own ourselves, that we can be the chief security officer of our life. So the moment circumstances begin to grow beyond our control, instead of taking shelter under the shadow of our God (Psalm 91:1) we begin to exercise fear and anxieties.

YOU ARE GOING TO BE MY MINISTER

I remember the very night I heard the voice of the Lord about the call of God for my life. On this very night, I heard on audible voice in my hear which said, "You are going to be my minister." Such news like this would have thrown somebody else into joy and great ecstasy, but not yours sincerely. Suddenly, my mind went to many Christian leaders who are doing well. I began to tell myself what else could I say or do that those had not done before? Why is He not making me a millionaire? With this I cast the whole thought to support His kingdom behind me and I vowed never to allow such a voice like this to deter my own life long goal. But the salient truth is, I dread ministerial work with all my soul, is it the lack and poverty that permeates the life of many of them. Or the demonic or the demonic opposition they are daily exposed to in the course of their duty. To really add salt to my injury, my father would always remind me of two or three pastors that were killed by witches and wizards. This coupled with other numerous "unforeseen" fears really kept me at bay, but this only prolonged my days of torment, affliction and suffering and this state of life never changed until I summoned some courage to stand before people to make a few speeches and gradually God began to send His help as I obeyed.

DO NOT CONCEDE "SIGNIFICANCE" TO THE DEVIL

I do not know what God has called you to do. Be it spiritual or temporal, you cannot afford to concede significance to the devil. The victory of any soldier on the war front is always hinged largely on the logistics given by the chief commanding officer. To willingly disobey his commander is to become a cheap prey in the hand of his enemy. So far, the torch bearer and leading officer have not shown any signs of fear or intimidation, which means it, has become a taboo in the life of his follower. Jesus Christ. He is the lion of the tribe of our race. He created fear itself and cannot be intimidated by His creation.

A missionary was following his guide through the thick jungle on his way to a new tribe. Time and again, they had to take their axes and literarily cut them away through the thick mass of growth.

Firstly, they come to an area where the growth was so thick that the sun was blotted over them and they were in near darkness. The missionary cried, "How are we going to find our way?" Calmly, the guide replied, "Sir, I am your Way." The same thing Christ is telling you in that crisis laden circumstance. I am your way. "I am the way, the truth and the life." (John 14:6)

Many of us are daily living in fear of what God has settled. Can you imagine Moses crying and wailing at the sight of the host of Pharaoh's army when God had given him the green light to move forward?

Due to fear:

- Millions of people cannot say the truth, as it is due to fear of men, while others could not break out of unholy relationships.
- Many cannot embark on a journey that will lead to their breakthrough.
- Many cannot answer the call of God in their lives due to fear of the unknown, most especially, when it is on a full time basis, even after they had heard or received clearly from the LORD.
- Some pastors have abandoned their altar while numerous are talking with both lips. (For God and for his enemy)
- Many cannot go ahead with their marriage plans.
- Many cannot take the risk of leaving their job for the one they really love due to job security.

- Many cannot enter into spiritual battle for their lives and for that of their loved ones for fear of satanic attack.
- Some ministers of God never offer deliverance prayer on their church members, even when such are at the mercy of the power or authority they claim to possess.
- Millions are daily soiling their hands with bribes in their offices not only because they want to please some high and mighty in some quarters but because they want to escape the ugly arm of poverty.
- Many are still attached to their family idols, shrines and non-biblical norms while some still secretly patronize herbalists and fake prophets.

FACE THE ODD AND BECOME THE LORD

God's utmost heart's desire is to raise men and women of higher standings for his people, people of grace, glory and candor, people of impeccable character, who are born not to repeat history but to re-write it, people who are not deterred but rejoices in making the names of their Lord known in the face of affliction, persecution and stiff opposition: people that have become a standard because of their standings for what they believe, to be living in fear is to be a burden to God and be useless to humanity.

You must know that anywhere God places you, either in your office, family or church, he wants to use you as His battle axes.

"Thou art my battle axe and weapons of war." (Jer. 51:20)

You are not a fool as people think. You may not be densely skilled, earthly smart and —extremely genius but you are God's representative. While I was working in a company, some of my colleagues were in the habit of stealing and looting company's goods to enrich themselves. One day, they decided to embark on a big fraud that was worth a fortune. Since, they knew they could not carry out such a big deal without my being notice of it, they decided to inform me and promised to share the largesse with me but threatened to deal with me if I ever tried to expose them. Immediately, I looked at all of them in the face and made my stand clinically clear and also affirmed that if they dared go in that direction, I would personally see that they all went down with it. It happened that whenever we were on night shift, at times we ate together. Meanwhile, they had decided to put a sedative drug in my food every night whenever I was on duty with them. So after we had our dinner around nine at night, I wouldn't know what else was going on around me until the next morning. This went on for some days, until I discovered their trick and decided to take the bull by the horns. The following night, I refused their food and I caught two of them in the act. Within a few days, their leader was sacked and the rest followed un-ceremoniously.

Friend, you are the only weapon left in the hand of your God, and you cannot afford to disappoint Him. He has made you a scarce commodity in a market place where everything goes, so you must discontinue living like a commoner.

Chapter 12

PRATICAL STEPS TO DEAL WITH THE SPIRIT OF FEAR

The various steps in dealing with a spirit of fear are as follows:-

- Deal with it as a spirit not as a type of temperament or nature.
- Understand its tricks/manners of operation in your life.
- Check your blood line to see if it is hereditary.
- Separate from every myth that makes you miserable.
- Memorize, meditate on the different scriptures on fear and believe and act on it.
- Fast, pray and wait upon the Lord for a direction or for a specific message.

FEAR IS NOT A TYPE OF HUMAN NATURE IT IS A SPIRIT

"For God has not given you a spirit of fear." (2 John 1:7)

One of the greatest deceptions of Satan is that fear has to do with our type of temperament and nature but from the word of God we can see clearly that it is not so.

Fear is never part of the making of man; fear was never a part of God.

So if the breath of God is that which makes man a living being, so anything that is less from a breath of God will automatically make a man "an ordinary being". Understand this, that fear was never in the dust neither was it in His breath so where did it come from? It came into man - from Satan - the moment he fell.

"And Lord God formed man of the dust of the ground and breathed into his nostrils the breath of life and man became a living soul."(Gen. 2 vs 7)

Always note that it was the breathe of life from God in a man that makes him a living soul, which means if fear is not from the bowel of God and is resident in you, what does that make of your soul? It makes you a dead soul. Hence, in every area of your life where you had been exercising fear, those are the areas where you are not experiencing a Godly kind of life. The intent of fear is to make you an ordinary being, so do not allow it.

UNDERSTAND ITS TRICKS AND MANNERS OF OPERATION IN YOUR LIFE

"For we have made lies our refuge, and under falsehood have we hid ourselves." (Isaiah 28:15e)

Spirit of fear operates more in darkness where they like to hide and to perpetuate evil, and it loves to hide itself under circumstances. Any one that daily experiences incessant fear on a daily basis surely needs a deliverance.

A sister came to me recently to report about how she had been having a great torment from the spirit of fear. I decided to take her up on deliverance and during the process I discovered that this strong demon in her is holding onto something. In my further investigation, I discovered she was once a prophetess in a white garment church and had been seen as their oracle. After revealing this to me, she said, "We don't appreciate her gift in our church, that the same spirit I'm trying to cast out from her is the same thing she had been using to bless her former church that is the end of the ministration."

Many people want to have freedom from the devil and still want to remain in their spiritual status quo, fear feed only on falsehood. The only way to deal with it is to be holy and walk in the light.

Having understood its tricks in your life, you may decide to do the opposite. For example, praying for 30 minutes or one hour without the light in your room is a way of helping yourself get rid of that spirit that says you cannot stay in the dark because something is hidden there that will harm you. Constantly and consciously do the opposite of what you fear, and within a short period of time you shall begin to experience a spiritual freedom from your captivity.

CHECK YOUR BLOODLINE

Many of us are only repeating the negative history that has been in our family for ages. Many of the problems we are facing may have been avoided if we had taken our time to examine the dominant weakness inherent in our family tree. Some family's sins are lying, sexual sin, alcohol, adultery, pride, cultic practices and idol worshiping. All these in a family are common grounds for Satan to breed freely. They are the secret behind the mystery of iniquity that has been hanging over many families.

A woman said she used to have a lot of fear and now she is beginning to see the same pattern in her daughter. The action you don't deal with seriously in your life will surely repeat itself in your children. Study your parents to see who among them has a trait of demonic fear in his or her nature. Are you going to pass the same demonic 'inheritance' on to your children or you will allow it to end with you? The choice is yours.

SEPARATE YOURSELF FROM EVERY MYTH THAT MAKE YOU MISERABLE

"Let no man therefore judge ye in meat or in drink or in respect of an Holy day, or of the new moon, or of the Sabbath day." (Col. 2:16)

Having received salvation, never allow culture to cut you short of God's glory again.

Family and society taboos are another secret of Satan in the life of many. Most of our culture and society's norms are mere extensions of satanic doctrine.

Fear of deities is not limited to Africans. For thousands of years, it has dominated nearly all mankind. In many parts of the world, almost every aspect of the people's life is directly or indirectly involved with some deity or with spirits. The mythologies of the ancient Egyptians, Greeks, Romans, Chinese, and others were deeply rooted in ideas about gods and spirits, which played an important role in personal and national affairs.

Besides these, people everywhere hare their superstitions and fears. In the West, breaking a mirror, seeing a black cat, walking under a ladder, and depending on where you live, Tuesday or Friday 13th are all viewed as omens foreboding something evil. In the East, the Japanese wear their

FEAR NOT

kimono with the left side folded over the right, for the other way is reserved for corpses. Their houses are built with no windows or doors facing the northeast so that the demons, which are said to come from that direction, will not find the entrance. In the Philippines, people wash their dead body's legs before burial service, so that "Saint Peter' will welcome them. Old folks tell youngsters to behave, by pointing out that the figure on the moon is "Saint" Michael, watching and writing down their deeds. In Nigeria, most especially in the West for example, it is said that a pregnant woman must not walk under the sun, so as not to be vulnerable to demonic children. For her to do so, she had to use safety pins with her clothes most especially her underwear. Again, there is the belief that nobody should eat at the entrance of the door, so that the food will be enough for you. You don't use bare hands to fetch water on a rainy day to avoid being killed by lightning. A new yam is not expected to be eaten until some oblations have been done to gods. Some parts of African nations see twins, dwarfs, and albinos as a demi god. Some don't even eat some kinds of fish, snails, snakes and some animals in their family.

These are all breeding grounds for demons of fear to thrive in people's lives.

"Wherefore if ye be dead with Christ from the rudiment of the world why as though living in the world subject to ordinances. Touch not: taste not, handle not, which all are to perish with the using after the commandment and doctrines of men." (Col. 2 v s20-22)

WORD MEDITATION

Word meditation is very important. If you prevail over the power and influence of fear, you need to know what the word says concerning each situation that is confronting you and declare them by faith, and then you need to exercise a lot of patience to allow the Holy Ghost to take you from one level to another.

FAST, PRAY AND WAIT UPON THE LORD

This is very crucial in every spiritual warfare. To have total breakthrough on this ground, you have to set time aside for this before the Lord.

This is not only a spiritual exercise, but a way of showing God that you are really ready to receive instruction and deliverance from Him.

Wait on the Lord: Be of good courage, and He shall strengthen thine heart: Wait, I say, on the Lord. (Psalm 27:14)

Chapter 13

YOU ARE A DIVINE SIGN

As a divine standard and a scarce commodity, that you are, you are not to be tossed about to and fro by the wind.

You are a champion with a divine backing, and every grace needed to break all forms of hindrance against your world has been made available.

Hence, we must realize that a Christian way is not 'a way' out of the world's harsh reality. There are challenges everywhere in our world, yet storms are not designed to make you stumble, they are meant to make you brainstorm in a new way so as to become a divine sign to your generation.

YOU EITHER CHANGE YOUR WAY OR YOU CHANGE YOUR NAME

A story was told of Alexander the Great who met a disreputable character whose name was Alexander. He looked at him face to face and said, "You either change your way or you change your name."

If you are a Christian and you are living like a chicken and vegetable, who do you resemble? How can you be sharing the same name with the Rock of ages and still be running away from rats, wall geckos, cobwebs, and mosquitoes in your room? How can you be complete in the head of all principalities and power and still be running helter-skelter from witches, wizards and familiar spirits?

And you are complete in Him, who is the Head of all Principalities and Power. (Col. 2:10)

God had made you a divine sign in the world to the high and the mighty, to the poor and the wealthy, to the kings and their subjects. It don't matter what you do, God has made you the head, you are not in the front to train your followers how to manage fear, sorrow, trouble and disaster. You are not redeemed to breed fear and confusion in people. You are in the front to confront. You are divinely impacted to show your generation a path to follow. It does not matter the level or position the people around you have attained, God has made you a plus to them not a minus.

GOD NEVER USES A CARETAKER BUT A RISK TAKER

Do you know that God never hands over His world into the hands of caretakers but risk takers? Men who will not allow the voice of reason to steal away their joy in their season.

Years ago, some of the members of our new branch where I pastored decided that we should go and greet the King in his palace to announce our arrival in the town and to give him a gift. On our arrival, the king who had been notified of our coming welcomed us warmly into his palace and after sharing some pleasantries with the king, I stood up to share the word, as it was given to me by the Holy Spirit, and I also prayed with him, his family, the land, his subjects and then we departed.

FEAR NOT

The next Sunday, a town member of the church who initiated our meeting with the king said that the king called her and said, "Did you reveal anything about our land, or myself to your pastor?" She said, "No, I just relayed the message to him the way it was given to him." He then said, "Why is he talking as if he knows what we are passing through including my personal case?" Right away, being a Muslim king, he promised her that he would be coming to our program at any time.

The question is if I had allowed fear to cripple my God given vision what would have taken me to the palace?

Maybe in contrast, I would have been there as a burden to beg not as a blessing to give. I would have even said to myself, 'Little me, what do I have to say before the king?' Remember, you a carrying the king of kings in your womb so you are incomparable to any king on earth. This our town king, despite being a Muslim not only promised to attend our church program but also promised to assist us in the land.

Thou therefore gird up thy loins, and arise and speak onto them all that I command thee, be not dismayed at their faces, lest I confound thee before them, for I have made thee this day a defensed city...... (Jer.. 1:17-18)

You have been made in Christ, so never allow a crisis to re-make you.

Thou therefore gird up thy loins, and arise and speak onto them all that I command thee, be not dismayed at their faces, lest I confound thee before them, for I have made thee this day a defensed city....... Jerem. 1:1718)

You have been made in Christ, never allow Crisis to re make you.

Chapter 14

FEAR NOT, YOU HAVE A BETTER STANDING

"And it was so, when the king saw Esther, the queen, standing in the court, that she obtained favour in his sight. And the king said unto her. What will thou, Queen Esther and what is thy request? It shall be even be given thee to the half of the kingdom (Esther 5:2-3)"

The very day, the king arrayed an ordinary girl, Esther, as his queen, she entered a new world not only in the palace but in all provinces under the king.

As a wife of the king of kings (Rev.19:7) you have gotten a unique standing on earth.

What does it mean to have a better standing? It is to have a special grace and favour before God, is to be unique and divinely clad with an outstanding aura from the presence of God. It is to be specially endowed with spiritual dignity and a special sign that reads, "Touch not". It is a way of casting a "lesser being" with a high degree of honor, putting him in the class of the untouchables, the unkillables, the undestrictables and the unconquerable.

"When I consider the heavens, the work of thy fingers, the moon and the stars, which thou hast ordained. What is man, that thou art mindful of Him, and the son of man, that thou visiteth him? For thou hast made him a little lower than the Angel, and hast crowned Him with glory and Honour. Thou makest him to have dominion and have put. All things under his feet. . . . . . (Psalm 8:3-9)

With your connection with God, you have become an extral being, and you have been empowered to rule and dominate over all things including your salient enemy, Satan.

In 2007, I was facing an issue that seemed to be taking a toll on my life and commitment to the things of God. My hope for a miracle was dwindling by the day, when the LORD spoke to me one day and said, "You have a better standing." I rose up from the floor and began to dance and praise God. A few weeks later, I got the miracle. As you are reading this piece, I don't know what you are facing right now, but I see God turning the tide for you. I see your change embracing you, and I see a new hope dawning for you, in Jesus name.

PEOPLE WITH EXCELLENT GRACE

...He had made them Kings and Priests and they shall reign on the earth (Rev. 1:6)

Have you ever pondered on the reason God himself decided to confer the title to kings (queen) and priest (priestess) to all his children? Do you ever ask why He never said, "I have made them man and woman and they shall reign on the earth?"

Anybody can be an ordinary 'human being' but being a human being only makes you an additional number to the people in the world. It never gives you a license to reign and to rule on the earth.

Since the beginning of the world to reign on the earth, you have to be among a special class of being. You must fall within the class of the peculiar people who are the most dominant force, on the earth.

What makes them peculiar?

Their divine stand makes them peculiar.

Haman would have done a lot of wrong things against common people and escaped the wrath of God but never with the people of covenant. (Esther 8:1-7)

He may have also gotten a lot of accolades and promotions through his violence acts and callous disposition to humanity but the very day, he stretched his might over the 'seemingly feeble' but un-common people, he met his waterloo. Jews are people noted with one God, they are never used to bowing to other gods. They can dance naked like David in front of their God and His people but never used to play around with 'fools'.

"And when Haman saw that Mordecai bowed not, nor give reverence, then was Haman full of wrath." (Esther 3:5)

From this day, I see every negative situation bowing at your feet, in Jesus name.

A brother recently was totally over whelmed by the thought of his house rent. His only hope which was his business suddenly crumbled and he was being daily coursed, chastened and threatened by his landlord to leave his premises. I was in his house praying on one Thursday morning; merely six days to the date given to him to vacate the house, when the Lord led me to raise him up from his kneel and said, "As you have been lifted up from the floor - so will God lift you up out of this trouble." According to him, he said due to the hopelessness of the case he never believed all my positive words on the situation - until that moment, when he summoned the courage to tell himself that if the servant of God said it, it means that is what it is going to be.

On Sunday evening around 5:00 - 6:00 in the evening, two different calls came into his cell phone that settled his debt.

A woman who had diabetes had travelled to the U. K. in Nov., 2011 for medical treatment but all to no avail, She could not stand for five minutes on her feet and untimely death seemed to be written all around her. A friend intimated us about her predicament, she was prayed for and the spirit of infirmity bowed before the Lord of Israel and she has been healed till date.

Months ago, the Lord led my path to a man's house, a transporter whose business had been grounded and he had been living at the mercy of his wife and friends for many months. He had become hopeless and totally out of tune with life. The Holy Spirit spoke expressly about his case and within a few weeks his money that had been "wickedly" put on hold by some people for years, was suddenly released. And he was able to get a vehicle to start his business again.

What have these people got in common? They are all people with a better and graceful standing with God; they are people that cannot be forgotten in shame, people in the mold of three Hebrew children that cannot be destroyed by intimidation or by fire. It does not matter how tense the wrath of the enemy against your family, business and ministry has been, it can never avert the glorious cause He had laid down for your destiny. In fact, I see all enemies hands on you working together for your bliss and comfort at the long run.

Terrorism may have killed millions around the world, but you can be at rest in your mind, you have been divinely exempted. You cannot be killed like a fool neither can you be cowed down under pressure, Why? Because you have a better standing with God. Your family joy cannot be short cut, your glory and life purpose cannot be stolen or be aborted. The fights of the enemy over your life and destiny cannot be sustained because their power and control over your destiny has elapsed. You might have cried before in the hand of your enemy, but that was then when God was processing you for success, but it will be a taboo for the weeping to continue for the time of oppression in your life has passed.

"They did cry there, Pharaoh, King of Egypt is but a noise, he hath passed his appointed time." (Jerem. 46:17)

LISTEN TO HIS VOICE NOT THE NOISE

For many of you who are passing through tough times and also thinking of how you will spend your eternity, what you need is to constantly listen to his voice and all shall be well. A few months ago, a middle aged woman shared this revelation with me. "I saw myself on a rugged narrow road, filled with sharp stones, ridges and contour. At the opposite of this path was a three lane road, beautifully garnished and well decorated with flowers. Those who are walking along this road seemed to be doing it aimlessly and pleasurably - talking, mingling and charting together on the way as they move with a lot of fun. As I was moving along this narrow way in pain, suddenly, I fell into a ditch which made me to protest bitterly to him who is guiding me on the way. He seems to say nothing except to encourage me to move on. I kept on moving with pain and discomfort, on the sharp stone and through the ditches and the contours until I got to a place where there was a big rock surrounded by a thick bush right at the center of the road. With this, I became so angry and I decided right there to cross over to the wide and smooth road after all, it is not painful to tread upon neither was it littered with sharp stones, ridges and contours like the narrow path. As I was pondering on this, I heard the voice of my guide saying, "Do not be discouraged, move on, as you have scaled through other obstacles in the past, so will you scale through this too." So, I summoned courage, and moved toward the rock.

FEAR NOT

As soon as I got to the bottom of the rock, I saw a tiny footpath that went towards the back of this rock, which meant some people had gone this way before. The moment, I scaled through to the back of this rock, I saw a big garden fenced all round. This fence had a little hole through which I was able to peep into the garden. Inside this garden, was a big beautiful building, which has a beauty and splendor that cannot be compared to any building on the earth. Immediately after I saw this, I heard my guide saying, "That is where you are going. That is your destination. Did I not tell you to be patient and that you would soon get there?" With this cheerful news, I became overwhelmed with joy and strength and my journey from this point forward became so painless and a comfortable one and I woke up."

What cheerful information for you and me on a rugged road. It does not matter what is going on around your world, only stick to His voice.

Terrorism in our nation is but a noise. Witches and wizards in your family are but a noise. Poverty in your life is but a noise. Sicknesses in your body are but a noise. Curses in your blood line are but a noise. It has passed its appointed time, brace up, and put on your strength.

Awake! Awake!! Put on your strength O Zion, put on your beautiful garment, Shake yourself from the dust. (Isaiah 52:1-2)

Beloved, don't stand for everything fear has come to give to you. You have to shake it away. You have a better standing with God. You are a people of his pasture. You are a walking grace in the land of the living, so stop fearing your future, stop fearing the enemy, and stop fearing the circumstances around you. (Ps. 91 vs 1-end)

You cannot die prematurely, you cannot be maltreated, or suffer loss of any kind without the permission of your heavenly Father. Let your mind be at rest. You are not only a divine sign but you also have a unique standing with God who created the heaven and the earth.

Chapter 15

WAR AGAINST THE SPIRIT OF FEAR

"For thou hast been a strength to the poor, a strength to the needy in his distress, a shadow from the heat, when the blast of the terrible ones is a storm against the wall. Thou shall bring down the noise of the strangers; the breach of the terrible ones shall be brought low." (Isaiah 25:4-5)

Whenever you are in captivity of fear, you are like the poor and the needy in distress, which needs a divine strength. You are like him that needs a comfort from a burning heat coming from a terrible one (spirit of fear).

Moreover, the Lord made you two promises here:

He brings down the noise of the strangers (He promised to neutralize the voice of that destructive fear around you).

The branch of the terrible ones shall be brought low which means all its tentacles networks and strongholds around your world will be uprooted permanently.

FEAR NOT

However, this calls for serious prayers. At this juncture, I humbly counsel that you separate three days apart, to stand in God's presence with fasting and prayer to deal with this demonic force called: The Spirit of Fear.

As the Holy Spirit of faith is real, so is the spirit of fear and until you deal with it, you cannot have access to your true glory.

Tag these three days, "War against the spirit of fear". These prayer points are divided into three meant for three days personal retreat, which can be in the form of night vigil or as your time permits.

The first two days, which is fifteen prayer points each is meant for each day while the third part is 70 general and selected prayer points meant to tackle all manners of evil manifestation –that is attached to fear in your life.

As you sincerely and faithfully take to this directive, I see the power of the Holy Spirit coming upon you a fresh – to break the yoke and grip of fear over your soul and give you a fresh breath of liberty and total freedom to walk in your God given DOMINION!

GENERAL PRAYER POINTS - DAY ONE

1. Lord, I thank you for redeeming my soul and for giving me salvation.
2. Lord, I exalt your holy name for preserving my soul till date from all strong and dreadful enemies.
3. I ask for forgiveness from every secret sin that is acting as a link and a door way to fear and I rededicate myself, in Jesus Name.
4. Hereby expose and neutralize every secret of the spirit of fear in my family, in Jesus name.
5. I expose and neutralize every secret of the spirit of fear in my spouse/children.

6. I expose and neutralize every secret of the spirit of fear in my life.
7. I pull down every altar and stronghold of fear in my blood line, in Jesus name.
8. I scatter every secret plan of Satan to steal my destiny through the spirit of fear, in Jesus name.
9. From today, I rise above every form of fear against my future, in Jesus name.
10. I break down every spiritual imprisonment of fear in my life, in Jesus name.
11. I neutralize every poisonous arrow of fear, shot into my soul through an ancestral power, in Jesus name.
12. I command every arrow of fear that had been shot into my system through a night dream to backfire, in Jesus name.
13. I release myself from covenant/curse which easily breeds fear into my soul, in Jesus name.
14. I terminate myself from every spirit of fear that steal away the glory of father, and terminate or cut short the progress, in Jesus name.
15. I bind and cast away every spirit of inferiority complex out of my life, in Jesus name.

GENERAL PRAYER POINTS - SECOND DAY

16. Lord, I thank you for redeeming my soul and giving me salvation.
17. Lord, increase my boldness and open my eyes to behold wondrous thing in your word for divine strength, in Jesus name.
18. Today, I bind every spirit of fear that entered into me in my mother's womb.
19. I command the fire of the spirit to destroy the force of fear that stand between me and the fulfillment of my vision, in Jesus name.

FEAR NOT

20. From today, I silence every evil force of fear that seeks to control me out of faith, in Jesus name.
21. I decree that every force of fear arranged to put me to shame and steal my joy be destroyed, in Jesus name.
22. I bind every spirit of fear sent by hell to steal my season, in Jesus name.
23. I am a child of glory, so I decree: Every force of intimidation and fear against my divine strength and glory. Bow! In Jesus name.
24. From this day, I walk out from the realm of fear into the realm of faith and trust, in Jesus name.
25. I shield my spouse and children from every arrow of fear, in Jesus name.
26. I command every strength/glory the spirit of fear had stolen from me to be restored right now, in Jesus name.
27. Replace the fear of Satan and the fear of men with the perfect fear of God, in Jesus name.
28. In Jesus Name, every knee shall bow, I therefore bow every goliath threatening me and blocking my way from crossing to the other side, in Jesus name.
29. I bind every spirit of fear of darkness and untimely death, in Jesus name.
30. Father, soak me and my family in your blood and immune me against satanic enchantment and every dart of fear from today, in Jesus name.

GENERAL PAYER POINTS - THIRD DAY

31. Thank Him for His redemptive grace upon you.
32. Ask for forgiveness of every hidden sin, acting as a door way to a spirit of fear in your life.

33. Lord, I expose every secret of the spirit of fear in my family bloodline.
34. Lord, I expose every secret of the spirit of fear in my life.
35. Lord, I expose every secret of the spirit of fear in my spouse.
36. I pull down every stronghold of fear in my family bloodline, in Jesus name.
37. I scatter and destroy every plan of Satan to steal away my destiny through the spirit of fear, in Jesus name.
38. From today, I arise above every form of fear against my destiny and future, in Jesus name.
39. I break down every imprisonment of fear in my soul, in Jesus name.
40. Henceforth, I release myself from every torment of fear, in Jesus name.
41. Through the blood of the lamb, I release myself from every curse which easily breeds fear into me in, Jesus name.
42. Through the blood, I separate myself from every spirit of fear that terminates my parent's progress, in Jesus name.
43. Through the blood, I neutralize every deposit of the spirit of fear in my family bloodline, in Jesus name.
44. I bind and cast out every spirit of inferiority complex that is troubling my life, in Jesus name.
45. I pull down every wall of fear that stand between me and my glorious vision, in Jesus name.
46. From today, I silence every evil voice of fear that seeks to control my soul out of faith, in Jesus name.
47. Father, increase my boldness in you and strengthen me more to believe your words the more, in Jesus name.
48. Father, grant me grace to walk on the water of my life (frightening situations/issues) with boldness, in Jesus name.

49. I decree that every force of fear arranged to put me to shame, to manipulate me and steal away my joy be bind and cast down to hell, in Jesus name.
50. Bind and cast out every spirit of fear sent to steal away my fruitful season, in Jesus name.
51. I am a child of glory so I decree every force of intimidation and fear against my divine strength and glory to bow to the obedience of Christ, in Jesus name.
52. From today, I walk out boldly from the realm of fear into the realm of faith, in Jesus name.
53. Through the blood, I destroy every knowing and unknowing covenant between me and Satan that is acting as a door way to the spirit of fear in my life, in Jesus name.
54. This year, I shield my family from every darts and arrow of fear, in Jesus name.
55. I command all my possessions which the spirit of fear had stolen from me be restored in seven fold, in Jesus name.
56. Through the fire of the Holy Ghost, I serve every link between me and an agent of fear around me, which is making the spirit of fear to have access to my soul to haunt it, in Jesus name.
57. From this day, I replace Godly reverence in the place of fear of men or of Satan in my soul, in Jesus name.
58. I rise up to challenge every Goliath threatening me from crossing to the next level, to bow by fire. in Jesus name.
59. Through the blood of the lamb, I neutralize every enchantment of wizards, witches and Satanist against me and my family's glory, in Jesus name.
60. I release thunder and fire against every spirit of fear that manipulates/intimidates me away from my possession, in Jesus name.

61. I bind and cast out to hell, every spirit of fear that is haunting my soul with untimely death and giving me a picture of sickness, failure and lack of progress on each step I take, in Jesus name.
62. Father, reveal more of your hiding revelation of yourself to me through your word to strengthen me in my inner man and in my spiritual course.
63. I soak my family and me in your blood as an immunity against every dart of fear, in Jesus name.

SELECTED PRAYER POINTS - MARITAL ISSUES

64. I bind and cast away every spirit that is making a marriage decision intimidating steps for me to take.
65. I soak my wedding date in the blood of the lamb, and cast away every evil spirit planted to make my D–day a negative one, in Jesus name.
66. I bind and cast out every spirit of delay that operate in my parent marital life and child bearing from interfering in my own life, in Jesus name.
67. I come against every evil prophecy that have been spoken against my marriage, in Jesus name

FEAR OF INSECURITY

68. I destroy every altar of evil establish against me in the spirit realm by fire, I pull down every stronghold against my peace and total security by fire, in Jesus name. (Duet. 7:8)

UNTIMELY DEATH

69. I neutralize the yoke of death hunting my soul, in Jesus name.

70. I silence the voice of the dead that is constantly haunting me in my sleep, in Jesus name.
71. I separate myself from all links between me and my dead ancestors by the blood of Jesus. (Ps. 118:17)
72. Through the blood of the lamb, I destroy every satanic coffin prepared for me, my spouse and my children, in Jesus name. (Ps. 49:15)

CHILDREN (PSALM 127:4)

73. I destroy all satanic ploy to make my children a source of sorrow instead of being and arrow, in Jesus name.
74. Every hellish ploy to make them a disgrace, instead of them to be a voice at the gate is hereby destroyed completely by fire! In Jesus name.

SICKNESS / DISEASES

75. By His blood, I revoke every spirit of infirmity in my family bloodline, in Jesus name.
76. Because I have been redeemed by the blood, I hereby revoke every health threatening schemes against me and my family, in Jesus name. (Deut. 7:15)
77. I decree that from today, divine health is restored to me, in Jesus name. (Jer.30:17)

NIGHTMARES

78. Because the head of all principalities and power has won the battle for me – I hereby scatter and neutralize every satanic injection through my dreams, in Jesus name. (Col. 2:15)

79. I bind and cast out to hell every dream manipulating spirit, monitoring and haunting me around, in Jesus name.

STAGNATION/POVERTY

80. Because my Lord crossed over to the other side, I hereby cross over to my next level, in Jesus name.
81. Every spirit of fear that always hinders me from taking bold and daring steps for my God is hereby destroyed by fire, in Jesus name.
82. I renounce every fear of men, which breeds mediocrity and stagnation in my life, in Jesus name.
83. Every foundation of limitation in my bloodline which easily besets, intimidates, and controls me on my way to major progress.
84. I consume every satanic fear that constantly fills me with fear whenever I'm travelling on the road, on the sea and in the air by fire, in Jesus name.
85. I bind/cast out to hell every spirit that constantly reminds me of how many accidents that has occurred. PREGNANCY (EXO. 23:26)
86. I destroy every fear of delayed conception in my family bloodline, in Jesus name.
87. Every plan of hell, complication and all negative distractive during delivery I hereby renounce and reject through His blood, in Jesus name.

OFFICE/JOB

88. I consume every satanic ploy that wants to put me in confusion and to frustrate me from my official position by fire.

89. Every negative lies and negatives voices against my official position and my personal business is hereby terminated by fire.

90. I decree that all that have dug an evil hole for me in my place of work to fall headfirst into it; I command every grave the enemy has prepared for my career and business to become their permanent burial site, in Jesus name.

91. I cover my office and my job with the blood of the lamb. With the blood, I revoke every strange tongue of fake prophets and soothsayers. I renounce every evil enchantment and neutralize all powers of divinations against the progress of my works/jobs both socially, financially and spiritually, in Jesus name.

Expecting your transformational testimonies!

Give Your Life to Christ Now!

If you have not given your life to Christ, it is pertinent to give it a thought now. This is necessary not only to make this piece meaningful to you but because we are at the zero hour and to help you escape the peril of hell.

If you are ready, please pray this prayer with me.

Father, I believe I am a sinner and you have shed the blood of your Son for my cleansing on the cross of Calvary to atone for my sins. Forgive me of my sin today and write my name in the book of life, in Jesus name, I pray. (Amen).

Segun T. Obadimu

COMING BOOKS FROM THE SAME AUTHOR

Taming Generational Curse

160 Inspirational Words for the Champion Vol.1 and 2

Superiority of Gift to Talent

Generational Leaders

The Benefits of Death

COMING BOOKS FROM BEULAH'S WORLD OUTREACH MINISTRIES

(An Arm of Glorious Ark Bible Church)

Divine Parables, Vol 2

Generational Leaders

The Benefits of Death

Superiority of Gift to Talent

Divine Acronym

Great Invitation

Giving your life to Christ is a must now, NOT only to escape an end time venom or to escape the fiery fire of hell but to live a life of dominion on the earth and also live with Christ forever!

If you are ready, pray this prayer with me.

"Lord, I am a sinner and I believe you have come to shed your blood for me on the cross, to wash my sins away. I ask that you forgive me ALL my sins, today and write my name in the BOOK of LIFE, in Jesus mighty name I pray."

Please, try and join a BIBLE based church where your faith will be further equipped and nourished with a pure WORD of GOD.

For personal counselling, prayer or if you're led to be a part of our Kingdom Partners, contact us at Segunobadimu2016@gmail.com

07038877885, 08030815350, 08093530663

Segun T. Obadimu

www.ingramcontent.com/pod-product-compliance
Lightning Source LLC
Chambersburg PA
CBHW052113070526
44584CB00017B/2457